Somewhere Within

J.S. Jerome

BookLeaf
Publishing

Presentation by *BookLeaf Publishing*

Web: www.bookleafpub.com

E-mail: info@bookleafpub.com

ISBN: 9789357440226

First edition 2023

I dedicate this collection to those unaware of their voice and to those not quite ready to share. I look forward to reading your stories one day.

ACKNOWLEDGEMENT

To Bookleaf Publishing, for the opportunity, for the challenge

To my inner circle (you know who you are) for reading and editing and encouraging and keeping me accountable...come hell or high water, this will have been a bucket list success

To the high and lows along the journey, you made for good writing

PREFACE

Writing has always been cathartic for me, a way to string carefully chosen words together to evoke emotions, all the while processing my own. And perhaps, that is where the apprehension stemmed from, for so long. The apprehension to share my words beyond my inner circle. Writing is incredibly vulnerable and at times, terrifying. But in the vulnerability comes the honesty, the beauty, the pain, the reality. That is my hope as you journey through these pages, whether it be from start to finish or pieces along the way, to find the vulnerability. And perhaps, just maybe, find your voice too

Somewhere Within

Where
do I
begin?

At the beginning or
somewhere within?

The path ahead was forged from the path behind
so is it truly the beginning or

just a continuation of a line?

Can I really say I start from scratch,
when who I am, I can't quite detach
from where I've been or who I was
or the times I won or the times I lost

Can I really dismiss the lessons learned
from those before me and the wisdom they
earned,
from overcoming challenges and conquering
fears,
from moving to new places and all those tears

Can I really overlook the footprints I see,

thinking somehow they don't belong to someone
farther along than me

Can I really let arrogance overshadow the path,
leaving me blinded,
worse,
holding me back

Whether at a beginning or somewhere along the
way,
I'll honor my past into my present as a future I
lay

Haze

I miss you

The crisp autumn breeze makes it hard to hold
on to the bag filled with popcorn seasoned with
chili to warm me up from the inside out

The chair across fashions itself into a hazy
image of you, the wind whipping your hair,
covering your smile at a terrible joke I've told

With my camera ready, I snap candids of you, a
most certain failed attempt to forever capture
this moment but a fond memory nonetheless

You would have loved every moment of this and
it makes it even harder as the cold snaps me
back to reality

I miss you

I miss the long drives and endless conversations

I miss the adventures and routine moments

I miss you, as I look away from the chair and
you slowly fade into the warm colors of the trees

Not "I'll miss you", as in a state of future being,
with a tinge of hope that one day we will return

But "I miss you", a current state of being that
will never truly vanish, only perhaps wane, a
state of being that will mistakenly see you in my
present, even though you will now only be in my
past

Haikus of Sorts

5

Sparse clouds, the sun shines
Like the trees, provide relief
Along the journey

Rain, soaking the earth
Like my tears, soaking my shirt
Hopeful new will grow

The hum of the car
Drowned out by the silence that
Nature resonates

Late night, bar shift ends
My shadow and I alone
Find solace, peace, here

Soon

I let go too soon

One more day,
one more hour,
one more minute to stay

And do the silly things couples do, finessed our
way

Even though deep down I knew one day would
be our last

still

I let go too soon

Despite the internal battle of want and right
I fought for the sake of others, instead of my
Own heart, in a way feeling I had no choice
Because deep down I knew I wouldn't be
Able to stay and

yet

I let go too soon

Never to be that singular entity in love
So I wanted to give you the best chance of that
And make sure you weren't left alone
Knowing deep down I knew we could not

but

I let go too soon

But such is life, the story of love and loss
Forbidden loves, hopelessly romantically, star
crossed
Who must drift apart to different shores
Hopefully forgetting the pain of what could have
been more

It doesn't make it easier,
it doesn't hurt less,
to let you go my love but promise me this

You'll fight for what you deserve and nothing
less
Which I know is unfair to say
Especially with both of us still feeling so intense

I know I will have to let go, tis the nature of our
story

I will let go

just

soon

Known

The air feels different here as it passes through
my nose, slowly filling my chest, bringing new
life to dead spaces

The murmur of the crowd, filled with nature
lovers and first time tourists, clicks of canes and
squeals of children, is drowned out by the
majesty of this place

We pale
in comparison
to this beauty

Time moves slower here, like a birds eye view,
the world far bigger, of which we can so easily
forget

I am halted, as though my feet know, the ground
on which I walk is not meant to be trodden
hastily

One can understandably feel lackluster in a place
like this,
lost even,
as though they don't matter

But it's in this majesty, this beauty, the most
unexpected of feelings wells within me

I am fully known

I am wholly known

For despite this majesty, this beauty

Where divine words carried existence in each
syllable

The power of "let there be" yielded complete
and perfect designs

The Speaker of those words chose to kneel down
and take from what He had made to make me

To attend to every detail, every intricacy, every
nuance

To fashion every part of me to capture a part of
Him

And when all was said and done, He moved in
just a little closer and His very exhale
commanded life

Slowing filling our chests, bringing us to life

My feet finally release me from this holy
moment, allowing the beauty around me to
propel me forward

Leaving me only able to exhale, the release all
the worship I can muster in this moment

Labels

We crave to be understood,

to be known

Yet we find the art of conversation too
vulnerable
Where listening has reduced what is being
spoken
to simply changes in air pressure hitting our ears
and the impatient waiting for that to cease so we
can be equally unheard

We seek answers and language to define us and
explain us with (label-less) labels
But the more labels we reject, the more we
create
And in the end, we become

less known and

less understood

Crown

I used to fear you

This scary monster that would contradically
grow, not by water but by air

Making not what I tried to do scary but what I'd
look like after

No one could know your true nature, you had to
be tamed

Every resist would be combat with fire,
neutralizing the bonds, rendering you limp

But that was the necessary standard, in order to
fit in

Because Beauty said you weren't good enough,
Beauty said you were unkempt

Little did I know how much you were suffering,
simply because I refused to say no

No to standards that made no sense, that never
truly embraced the world around

Until enough was enough, the tears, the pain, the
scars

You weren't the monster I thought you were but
just different and trying to shine

I slowly coaxed you out of the cave I shoved
you in, learning to care and tend and love

Until one day, in all your glorious wonder, you
sprung out

To be the crown I had been missing, all this time

Bridge

I teeter on the edge of a bridge, built of my own making

Misshapen stones, cemented with tears and frustration

At times almost too sharp to step on but in the pain, hope, that it propels me forward

There is a light off in the distance, steady and true

I continue to build towards it but my eyes remain on what's behind me,

Pavers of disappointments and unmet expectations

Reminders of yesterdays that have lead to unanticipated todays, leaving tomorrows all the more unknown

Alone I toil, for this is my journey, is it not? A journey I must walk alone?

Like a fog, life has clouded the original plan,
one I've seem to have forgotten

Where taking on the burden to build seems
easier and charting my own course seems wiser

But the more I build, the no closer I get

So maybe it's time for me
to just stand still

And in the moment I do, the fog begins to lift
and the burdens I've carried feel oddly lighter

And by my side, I see the ultimate Builder,
making smooth the stones that once hurt me

He stretches out His hand, scarred from work
only He could do

But there is no pain in His eyes, only love and a
smile I feel like I've always known

He brings me closer, deep into His side

"Where did you go?" He asks, "Where were
you, my sweet child?"

I collapse in His arms, finding safety in His
voice

"You are safe at last, you were found, you are no
longer lost"

And the light I fought so hard to build towards is
now the Light, by my side, leading me forward

Glass

At times I might shatter, at times I might bend

At times you can see right through me and at times I may be a lens

You can take me and mold me into the smoothest of marbles

Or you can break me into pieces, each fracture reflecting a unique sparkle

The heat makes me malleable, allows new shapes to form

It can also take what I once was and allow new properties to be born

I'm an unusual medium, both with great risk and great reward

So many facets still yet to be explored

And as you ironically look at me and see what I can be put through

You might be surprised to see this medium is
you

Sonder

I can't be the first
Not to suggest I think I am
But what was it like for, back then,
feeling things you shouldn't

What was it like being in a room, around a
person, within reach but you couldn't touch

Or if you did, as a person of faith, what was that
journey like?

What was faith like back then?

Was it a tug of war of passion for the Word in
the midst of forbidden love?

Did you have confidants to pour over the truth
with, in the midst of the struggle?

Giants of old seem so different, sojourners of the
golden age seem so silent, wanderers of the
present age seem so...

I find myself in a sonder

Why

Why do you hate me for the color of my skin
Or is it something much worse, rooted within?

The fiber of your being, to your very soul
Is it there that you still hold fast to the lies of
old?

That somehow said, simply because of my skin
I was ugly, worthless, forever less than

That I could never think or learn or read or write
And that no matter the wrongs you did to me,
you were always right

I've never understood how you can carry such a
load
For hate and anger will only lead you down a
dangerous road

I'm sorry you'll never see what I am capable of
And to live out God's truths of faith, hope and
the greatest of all, love

But rest assured, I won't let you rob me of who I
am

Let it be known, right here, right now, I am
taking my stand

Dusk, Dawn

I walk across the room, nearly floating, as to not
disturb the quiet around me, a quiet gently
harmonized only with the flicker coming from
the bright red hearth

The aroma tickles my nose as I bring the cup to
my face, the steam whipping around, obscuring
my view, the warmth of the tea slowly radiating
through my hands

The weight of the day gradually dissipates, as I
finally sink into the colorful pillows around me,
instinctively bringing my legs closer to my torso

A heavy sigh escapes, from a breath held longer
than I realized, leaving me more aware of this
needed rest

My gaze drifts to the treeline, as the pinks and
purples intensify with the approaching dusk,
marking the end of another day, another chapter

Leaving me to sit in the space in between, the
space that forces a pause, a reset

Breathing space

Where thoughts and words and dreams are not
racing for completion but pace just enough to
enjoy the moment

And allow you to bask in the break you've so
desperately needed

Fully releasing your held in breath, to make
room to take in the anticipation of what is to
come

The mystery of the unknown, the unsure
but brimming with unmet potential

The day ends, the fire dies, the tea's consumed

But a new dawn, a new chapter is on the horizon

(Not So Random) Thoughts

Stop inspecting the wall in front of you
when there is a door right beside you

The accidental roads you find yourself on
might be the intentional roads to your
destination

There is pain in staying the same and
there is pain in changing

-

pick the one the moves you forward

Sometimes

Sometimes the most basic of questions will yield
the most profound of answers

Where "How was your day?" or "Did you eat?"
will build bridges instead of walls

Sometimes the most basic of behaviors will
yield the most peaceful of actions

Where two attentive ears will allow for the
successful transaction of two useful cents

Sometimes the most basic of gestures will yield
the most precious of alliances

Where a smile and a nod can make one
remember they are not alone

Sometimes it's the basics, the things we can so
easily forget

That will restore the simplicity and joy of
humanity

Phantom

Smooth

the subtle crescendos and rollbacks,

the melodic cascade that ever so gently flows

carrying sweet nothings and unspoken dreams

Striking a chord from the ear to the heart

A harmonic felt across heartbeats

A home found in the depths of the swirls of deep
brown and flecks of gold, growing brighter the
longer I look

Unfathomable when my heart will find another
song such as yours

Or find a safe haven as warm and endless

Time does little to break the hold of the now
phantom buzz

My phone feeling heavier and heavier, fully
charged yet seemingly lifeless

Knowing you won't, you can't but nonetheless,
my hope remains unmoved

2020

i
am
tired

i have written these words a thousand times and
a thousand times no change

i take one step forward towards rest only to feel
the chain of fatigue tighten around my ankle

the chain that grows bigger and stronger and
heavier with every word, every text, intended to
love but instead lashes and tears and rips my
back, as i crouch to protect against one more
blow

there is only so much i can take

the weight of the past, of the present, of the
future,
all distorted,
slowly suffocates,
leaving me lightheaded and disoriented,
stumbling towards the light, in spite of the
growing throb, hoping to find clarity

i crawl with any strength i have left

my hand lands on a bolt cutter, fashioned by words
stronger than the pain,
stronger than the chains

i don't know the strength of it but i wield it anyway,
fighting fiction with truth,
pain with purpose,
destructible with indestructible

before i can even cut, the chains disappear and i
see clearly how far i've come,
in spite of the load i carried

and the cutters become a mirror, not to see the
reflection of what others say but the image of the
One i bear, and who knows my name

Journey

I fear permanence,
definitive plans where definites are never
guaranteed.

Where life can crawl
then sprint
then fall,
all before the sun sets.

My plans breed what ifs and who knows, like a
hamster on a wheel, the dread of the tread,
milling through life, uncertainty leading to
stagnancy,

stuck

but still stretching towards goals that feel
unattainable,
dreams that feel unreachable

But

There is a fight.

Through the sands of time, quickly sucking us
in,
there is a tremble.

Deployed from the heart, on a march to the
mind, activating nerves and signals and resolve.

A tremble that pulls through the mire, that
pushes through the mold of words that have
created a shell of you,

a facade to the world only to have you hidden
within, chipping away.

But the Word inside of you is greater and
stronger and bears the keys to break you free to
see the dreams, meant for you, meant for me.

Permanency

Is not for me.

But no longer from fear of the unknown but
certainty of the destiny that only comes through
the journey.

So
walk on,
push on,

fight on,
journey on

Until We Meet Again

Until we meet again, may the memories of me
be fond

May the days we spent leave a smile on your
face and the warmth of the hugs linger on

Until we meet again, may what comes be devoid
of fear

May the dreams we have fuel the steps we'll
take and be the strength to fight for what's dear

Until we meet again, may today be filled with
felicity

May the present moment be embraced and all
that it entails met with tenacity

For you see, until we meet again

You and I will be

Somewhere within